HAL•LEONARD
INSTRUMENTAL
PLAY-ALONG

AUDIO
ACCESS
INCLUDED

PLAYBACK+
Speed • Pitch • Balance • Loop

T0084233

CELLO

PIRATES OF THE CARIBBEAN

To access audio visit:
www.halleonard.com/mylibrary

4530-3958-9755-1878

ISBN 978-1-4234-2204-4

WALT DISNEY MUSIC COMPANY

DISTRIBUTED BY

HAL•LEONARD®

7777 W. BLUEMOUND RD. P.O. BOX 13819 MILWAUKEE, WI 53213

Visit Hal Leonard Online at
www.halleonard.com

Title	Page

THE BLACK PEARL

CELLO

Music by KLAUS BADELT

small notes optional

BLOOD RITUAL/
MOONLIGHT SERENADE

CELLO

Music by KLAUS BADELT

DAVY JONES PLAYS HIS ORGAN

CELLO

Music by HANS ZIMMER

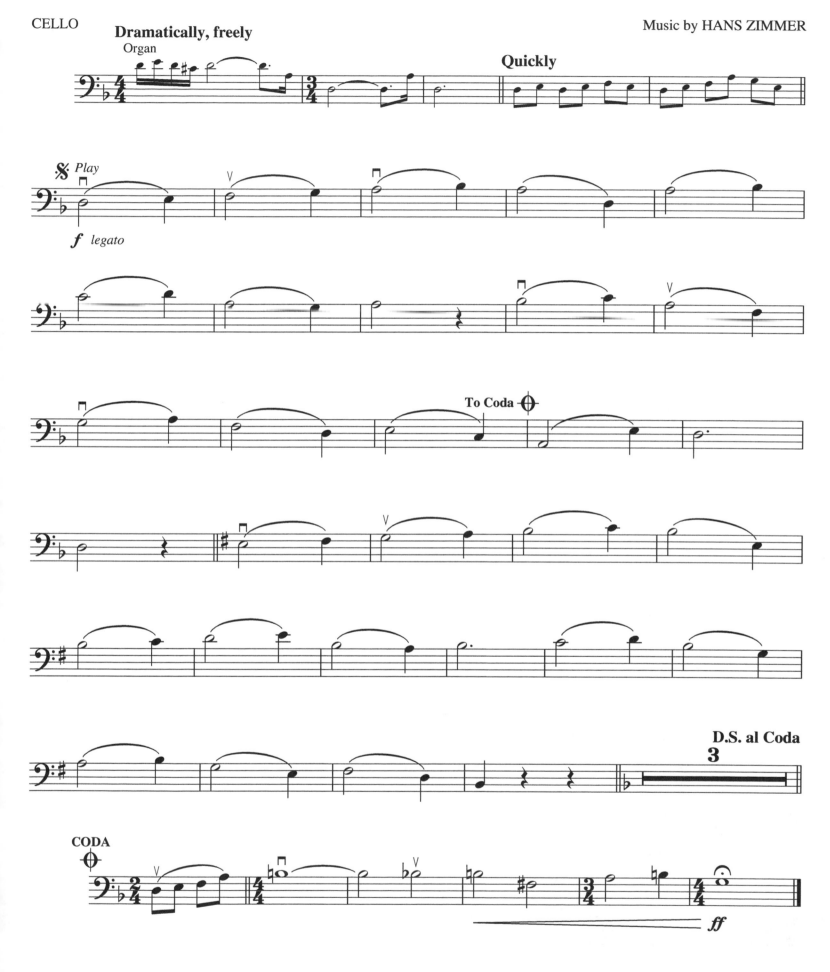

DAVY JONES

CELLO

Music by HANS ZIMMER

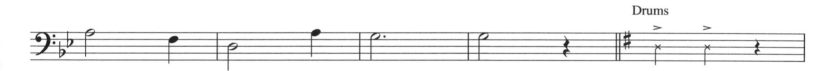

DINNER IS SERVED

CELLO

Music by HANS ZIMMER

I'VE GOT MY EYE ON YOU

CELLO

Music by HANS ZIMMER

HE'S A PIRATE

CELLO

Music by KLAUS BADELT

JACK SPARROW

CELLO

Music by HANS ZIMMER

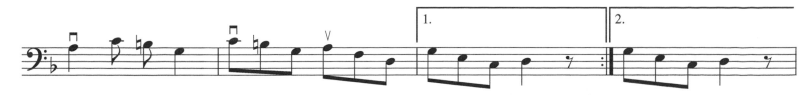

THE KRAKEN

CELLO

Music by HANS ZIMMER

THE MEDALLION CALLS

CELLO

Music by KLAUS BADELT

ONE LAST SHOT

CELLO

Music by KLAUS BADELT

TO THE PIRATE'S CAVE!

CELLO

Music by KLAUS BADELT

TWO HORNPIPES
(Fisher's Hornpipe)

CELLO

By SKIP HENDERSON

WHEEL OF FORTUNE

CELLO

Music by HANS ZIMMER

UNDERWATER MARCH

CELLO

Music by KLAUS BADELT